My Side of the River

My Side of the River

Poems by

Gae Alexander

For my sweet friend Sandy — With Love, Rebecca/Gae

© 2019 Gae Alexander. All rights reserved. This material may not be reproduced in any form, published, reprinted, recorded, performed, broadcast, without the express written consent of Gae Alexander. All such actions are strictly prohibited by law.

Author photograph by Janet Taub

Cover design by Shay Culligan

ISBN: 978-1-949229-37-0

Kelsay Books
Aldrich Press
www.kelsaybooks.com

*For Stephen, for Lauri and Richard,
and for Alex and Katie—my dear ones all.*

Acknowledgments

My warm thanks to all the poets who have provided insights, suggestions and encouragement in poetry workshops and readings over the years, and to the many playwrights I worked with during my years in the theatre. All are accomplished and dedicated to their craft and all have influenced my writing. A special thank you to poet Doris Henderson and the Danbury Chapter of the Connecticut Poetry Society. I also thank poet James Scrimgeour and the New Milford, CT Commission on the Arts for awarding first prize to two poems in this collection, "This Already Was Dreamed" and "Observance", in poetry competitions. Thanks to Lou Rodgers and Golden Fleece Composers Chamber Theatre in Manhattan for including poetry readings among their artistic offerings for decades. Finally, my gratitude to Don Anderson for bringing my work to the attention of Kelsay Books.

Contents

If You Will	13
Doing	14
As It Happened	15
February Morning	16
As If God Were Grieving	17
Wild Violets	18
Should I Be Blue?	19
View from a Cheap Seat	20
This Already was Dreamed	21
Augury	23
Day and Night	24
In Darkness	25
When Everything I know Is Not Enough	26
Amaranthus	28
Traveler	31
The Turkey Tree	32
At The Temple Of Sináwava	33
On This Splendid March Morning	35
Memory from a Parched Place	36
When the Least of Us	38
New York City, Thursday September 13th	39
Self-Centered Exercise	40
Arithmetic	42
Out of the Night	44

14th Autumn	45
In May after Rain	46
Rerun	47
When Last I Held Your Hand	48
A Coming To Mind	49
Observance	51
Heartsong	52
Bounty	53
Jasper	54
Bestowals	56
Light	57
November 19th, 1:35 p.m.	58
Take My Love	59

If You Will

Take my heart. Like flint it contains
the possibility of fire. Strike it
against the coldest, hardest stone.
Do it again, again, again, until
nothing in this world can prevent
a cascade of sparks like a hundred falling stars
thrilling the blackest night.
Ignite something then, a thing

sure to be beautiful in its burning,
as love is beautiful in its burning;
as even the pain of being consumed
in the fires of love is beautiful.
When that is done and the blaze
is climbing high,
draw me close, friend, to the flames.
Let me feel the heat.

Doing

Things need doing.
Dishes after dinner,
or the porch needs sweeping
mornings after brisk
night winds.
My doing and doing for
is part of loving life;
loving all whom I love.
Recalls early years
when my doing was more for you.
Our years of burning at the core
for each other.   Desire
fierce as a fresh abrasion,
healed by losing
and finding ourselves
in each other's bodies;
by falling fathoms down
in love's umbral oceans,
finding at those depths
dark gleamings
like prayers in the night.

As It Happened

It began with the mundane,
sweeping autumn scatter from the patio.
A gathering wind whispered from the trees,
Your task is futile. As proof, one great gust
sent shivers through branches

to launch an avalanche of leaves:
maple, oak, ash, in saffron, apricot, burgundy,
cascading like a dam had burst,
catching at my hair, my sweater, grazing my cheeks
with the delicacy of kisses, not lustful but tender.

Good, my letting go.
Good, dropping to my knees,
gathering handfuls to hold above my head,
opening my fingers so to see them fall
again, again, with God or the wind confirming,

For you this moment, this gift,
this rapture of leaves.

February Morning

This day resembles nothing so much
as an old photograph of itself.
Nothing moves. Breezeless, the trees
hold their ground like sculpture.
Morning is stunned
by hard angles of ice-white sun.
Two *bouffant* blooms, desiccated blossoms
of last year's hydrangeas,
keep their clutch on bare thin bone.
The branches can't recall them anymore
and yet not one of the onion-skin
petals lets loose. No squirrel
breaks and runs, purposeful,
over the dormant grass. No bird
turns overhead or lights
in the granite-color trees.
Houses on the hill across the valley
sit squat, closed, inscrutable.
No joy, no heartache
ever will escape to tell a thing.

As If God Were Grieving

Such endless weeping from the wretched sky.

Rain is flung against the pane.
Spherical at first, the drops
cling for one brief moment then
course along in streams of tears
down the glass and lose themselves
at the furrowed sill and spill to the ground.

This rain, like anguish not to be assuaged.

Wild Violets

Don't tell me they can't
   be happy.

They aren't sentient beings so they can't
   be happy?

Look at them! Their faces
   open, guileless,

pink and purple, cream and blue,
   looking for all the world

– what else could you call it? –

     cheerful.

What else can you think
   as they chastely

shimmy in the breeze,
   that chorus line of hundreds

on my April lawn?
   Who knows if they know they won't last long.

But hey, you can't tell me that while they're here
   they don't just love it.

Should I Be Blue?

Should I be blue that I never will
be able to soar in cyberspace,
never be adequate to this world
of exploding technologies –
a world that makes solitude anachronistic;
invites faceless strangers to lob
puerile, vicious insults back and forth
by means of electronic catapults;
finds ever new ways to make
deadly weapons deadlier?

If this were a serious question
I'd have a serious answer.
Serious answers are everywhere I look.

Take my yellow poppies for example,
unveiling their cheerful faces with the dawn,
humbly folding their petals when the sun sets.
Or start with the rising sun itself,
an aureate ribbon cresting the hill,
spreading soon like a golden shawl
to rest upon the shoulders of the day.
Or take the waning hours, the sun
little by little lowering itself
into the waiting river,

its amethyst, cinnabar, sapphire
floating on water, dissolving at last
in deference to the rising moon.

View from a Cheap Seat

Not a pop diva descending from the rafters
to the stage in a kaleidoscopic light show
like a sexy space alien with back-up dancers.
No frenzied crowd, no scalpers
on the sidewalk hawking tickets
to the tune of a small fortune.

Just a mother raccoon high in a gnarly oak.
I'm watching her from the patio.
She gave birth a few minutes ago.
How intently, up on that limb,
she cleans the cub of her fluids – blood,
and what's left of an amniotic sea,
waters which sustained its life inside her.
She must do this before she rests
for the sake of its sudden separateness;
the sake of its new need, her nipple.

I'm witnessing a spiritual act.
Instinct yes, I wouldn't argue,
but something sacred in it too.
I watch with an aching pleasure.
Later on I'll go inside, make tea,
think of times long past.

This Already was Dreamed

I hugged my arms and waited
on the hill overlooking the town.
I hoped the sun might grace
the close, impassive houses
with a lavender glance before leaving them
all to their true colors.

What broke with the dawn was the silence.
A flatbed truck the color of mold
gunned up Main, surely doing fifty,
took a hairpin turn at the top of the green
with a shriek, and whipped its load
right into the street. *Close call,*
I mumbled, thinking of the driver,
who disappeared with the truck.
Then I saw: All my things –
bookshelves, bed, the dining table –
dead where they fell, in peculiar positions,
angular, jutting, oddly beautiful.

This interests me, but …

I can't think now.
I must attend to the meal,
the bread and cheese and olives,
the wine, the figs,
I'm preparing to serve the three,
father, son and son-in-law,
who sit recondite in lotus position
there on my dining room floor.
They will not ask me to partake with them.

That saddens me, but …

I can't think now.

Shortly I must climb the stairs and pack
for the journey you and I will make by rail.
I will take the gossamer raiment designed for my tenderest flesh.
I will wear my hat with the purple plume
and my daintiest silk button shoes.
Tomorrow I will follow as you carry our bags

through car after car of a mile long train.
When you vanish, as you will,
in one of my blinkings,
the elderly conductor will think it strange
how you stole off the train two villages back,
taking my carpetbag with you.

This disquiets me …

but I can't. I can't think now about

what I will do then.

Augury

The tilt of my teacup this morning
was poignant, no other word, no

escaping the fact. Nor how sunlight,
chill and aslant, brittled and bleached

the look of leaves drifting down
in the yard (portentous pattern

on the grass later, leaves having fallen
just so). Then too, the way

your shadow leaned against the door.
In such manner I divined that love,

present and warm as a kitchen,
will take of me soon a cool leave.

Day and Night

By day
I keep forgiving you. I'm Charity.
I relinquish offense, wave upon wave, like an ocean.
I consider my own expectations.
Were they a sin against your singularity?

In my sleep
you lie heedless, naked on a beach.
I'm a great vicious bird of no special color.
I seize your soft belly with talons of razor.
I pluck out your eyes with my big hooked beak.

In Darkness

She had made her
   bed,
as they say. Must lie
   in it a lifetime

of slow suffocation.
   Often
she would rise, two,
   three a.m. He,

dreaming, never knew.
   Hers alone the night
alley for walking
   its length and back,

and again. Hers too, stars,
   scent of pine. Some nights
she fancied the air
   falling down the slopes

of Mount Timpanogos
   to be sighs of Sleeping Maiden.
They say Princess Ucanogos,
   the night she learned his body

lay slain on the valley floor,
   slipped her own,
left it recumbent
   atop the mountain

and never looked back
   as she rode the stallion wind
over moonlit cliffs, down shadowy canyons
   to him, her warrior lover.

When Everything I know Is Not Enough

Low, undulant, the hills across the river
are my horizon line.
They are topped with ash and oak,
sycamore and maple, all leafless now.
Over there is where the sun sets.
Against a neutral sky, branches,
small from here and fretted,
look to be an ancient form of writing.
They are hieroglyphs I study,

hoping to decipher lost wisdom
magically preserved in this manner
by priestesses when the armies
of Yahweh torched their temples.
Dormancy has exposed the shape
of the earth beneath the trees,
its secret face. Unlike them
in their austerity, it looks
surprised, a little abashed.

I recall the trees were bare
in my season of decision.
I recall his hands, how he held them
palms up; how he said, *I've learned
you're the only one for me;*
how I touched his cheek, wordless.
I recall his bafflement:
*What will you do alone
after all these years?*

                        What I do
is write this poem. The treetops keep
their secrets. They stand black at sunset
against the day's last blaze. Their answers
are not to my questions.

Moon slips into water.
The darkened window
frames my own reflection.
The sun will rise tomorrow
on my side of the river.

Amaranthus

Friends ask if she always loved best
the undeserving. She doubts it.
When names are named only his
carries the force of a hammer.

Out of their mouths or on her own lips,
it sometimes sounds like Judas. Yet,
for all the sorrow in his wake
she tells them loving him

was the making of her. Not – as she
feared in the scorching climate
of anguish and the later chilly
grayed-out season of the heart –

her undoing. In those tormented days
irony and symbol were hurled
at her head, dangerous debris
flung by unnatural forces.

Out of a gardening book the word
Amaranth flew at her face, shrieked
its other name: Love-Lies-Bleeding.
A pair of old marriage maples,

planted in the nineteenth century
by newly-weds when the house was theirs,
were parted by the death of one.
It fell to a chainsaw. And so on.

She murmured, *He never deserved
my love,* as if love benefits only
the loved, not the lover.
As if deserving were the point.

She called herself fool, love's fool,
cursed herself for finding love
hard to dispatch and forgiveness
elusive, short lived. In those days

love and forgiveness she took
to be one, not knowing only love
abides, while forgiveness requires
a thousand and one renewals.

In those days contradictions
ran amok, creating in her mind
a kind of cognitive dissonance,
rendering perception suspect:

Exercising judgment for her own sake,
she had left him. Surely
that was not the same
as passing judgment. Was it?

A fear grew that she never
had loved at all, for love endures
all things, according to Saint Paul.
Love bears all things; it never fails.

Life became something small
and still, a thing insensible
of necessity, a thing poised
to stop remembering itself.

But life in suspension is life,
nevertheless. There comes a warming,
a stirring. A sapling maple sprouts
where the old one was felled.

In it part of an old love
lives on. And memory admits
that Amaranth goes by many names,
including Everlasting.

Her love indeed had endured
all things, remaining with the loved
as a gift she could not withdraw,
as she had withdrawn her presence.

Thus the inconstant always will
receive the blessing of love,
and the givers of love will know
theirs is the greater blessing.

For loving always breaks the heart
open, and open, the heart
can take in everything:
all the world's suffering;

all the world's beauty;
and all the love that is offered
by others whose own good hearts
were broken open by love.

Traveler

Give me lushness.
Give me flowers too flamboyant
to be believed.
Bring mango, bring cream.

Perfume my hair with a spice
I cannot name. Braid it
with shells, tiny and blushing
and singing of pearl.

Give me silken breezes
to whisper my naked length
and leave me swept
sensuous as dunes on the shore.

Night-glide me through lagoons
overhung with leaves like fans
swaying in cool lunar light,
dappling my moon-bright face.

Then give me sun white hot.
Watch me ignite, burn
everything pleasureless
down to the bone.

Don't fear that I'll be
lost to the flames.
I know my way back
to where they play it cool.

The Turkey Tree

—Kanab Canyon, February 2006

A tower of fortitude rising in twilight.
A hundred years' patience
etched in its furrowed bark.
Winter bare but waiting, as always,
with gentle reaching boughs
anchored by a stout trunk.
Soon the first large arc
is carved on the dusk.
The first of them has soared
out and away
from the tooth-edged cliff.
It comes to the cottonwood's waiting arms
with a muffled slapping sound.
Another, then others, until
en masse they wheel, spiral, swoop,
hover a moment and find
perches for themselves.
A flock of wild turkeys,
two hundred, less or more,
settle for the night in the cottonwood.
As silhouettes against the waning light,
they are perfect foliage.
Great dark leaves
on this, the perfect tree.

At The Temple Of Sináwava

—Early March in Zion Canyon

Soon I'll be in the canyon's embrace,
I think, as I draw near
The Temple, a place
Where the canyon walls appear

Scarcely an arm's length apart.
Damp, fragrant, in springtime lush,
A place where waterfalls rush
To the river as to a sweetheart.

But around the final curve
A scene seemed set to unnerve:
An ambulance, where hikers hover
As stolid paramedics cover

A body that lies on a gurney.
I catch my breath, then turn away
And face the river. It's not my day
To think of final journeys;

To consider the fatal fall
Or when the heart might fail.
This is my day to be in thrall
To the riverbank, now pale

From a dusting of snow;
In thrall to the river itself, its low
Purling on the rocks. To be avid
For its silver curve, fervid

With love for ripples burnished
Like copper in four p.m. light.
I won't today forgo this sight,
For I am here and furnished

With a heart that still beats
And a soul that knows to prize
The beauty that still greets
These greedy living eyes.

On This Splendid March Morning

—Zion National Park

I devour this place:
its cotton candy clouds,
pillowy and sweet,
afloat in purest blue.

I devour this place:
its sheer rock walls,
amber and alveolate
as a honeycomb wedge.

I devour
the cinnamon sugar cliffs
that frame the sky.
And I devour

the sinuated mounds,
Navajo sandstone,
like huge scoops of ice-cream,
cherry-vanilla, about to melt.

I feast in this place,
this fine confectionary,
and drink in great gulps
of cedar-washed cold mountain air.

Memory from a Parched Place

> *Cruelty, like every other vice, requires no motive*
> *outside of itself; it only requires opportunity.*
> —George Eliot

Years ago I lived a while in the desert.
There one late fall day I saw a thing happen.
Out away from the highway, where battered
saguaros, old soldiers, defied relentless
invasions of dollar-eyed developers.
Out in the sage-scented stillness
where I'd gone to be able to hear
the questions in my head.

They ground the silence to dust, the men –
one young, a kid, the other not.
Their once-red pickup, muffler hanging,
turned off the road, sped my way, jolted to a stop
just yards from my spread blanket, my half-peeled orange, my
    confusion:
how fast to gather up, get out.
How to seem not nervous.

They gave me the eye as they jumped from the truck,
but turned to scan the ground; to search,
closely, as for something lost. Mere moments,
then *Yeah,* the older one grinned. *Yeah!*
They squatted on their cowboy-booted heels
at a tarantula's burrow, dangled at its door
a length of string they'd brought
to rouse the thing they'd come for.

Into, out of, in and out, teasing by inches,
invading the small nest.   *Holy shit, hold on!*
Face flushed, the young one took a blob of pink
out of his mouth. He caught my eye,
then went ahead and did it.
I knew as I left in my own cloud of dust:
The spider would writhe the rest of its life away
on a bubblegum wad at the end of a string.

When the Least of Us

Last year, I was stunned when a 30-year-old woman in North Kivu had her lips and ears cut off and eyes gouged out after she was raped, so she couldn't identify or testify against her attackers. Now, we are seeing more and more such cases.
—*Anneke Van Woudenberg, Congo Specialist for Human Rights Watch*

How can we bear to wake on mornings
when the last words on our lips
in the dark of night
were, *God, save Your world
from the inhuman savageries
we humans commit upon each other!*

But the planet is still here for now,
so we rise to the dear small comforts
of coffee and our daily tasks,
and wonder why it should be we whose hearts
are lifted when the sun burns through clouds,

or we catch from somewhere a strain of melody;
why it is we who get to thank God for daily bread
and the blessing of ordinary days
when the least of us His children,
they who suffer most the horrors of His world,
are surely as deserving.

New York City, Thursday September 13th

—to those who perished Tuesday, 9/11/01

Involuntarily I breathe.
Involuntarily you ceased to breathe.
Today I wander somber downtown streets.
The air is oppressive, unnatural.
As I walk I inhale,
involuntarily,
the fine particulate of you,
last of your mortal substance,
invisible now.
I consider your final breaths.

My wild-eyed mind casts them as doves,
visible in my wild mind's eye
above the gouge in the skyline.
A stunning great flock soaring high
above the sirens keening,
beyond the reach of rising smoke,
beyond the reach of any tower,
beyond the reach of anything except –
should God be there and listening –
a forlorn nation's prayers.

Self-Centered Exercise

Another day, another headline
shrieking bloody murders; savageries
in too many countries to count.

Like a mad king giggling as he signs
his own death warrant, the world is set
to preside over its own demise

from wars and the poisoning of Earth.
I ache for the multitudes lost,
for multitudes that will be,

while knowing that to say *I hurt*,
at this remove from their pain,
is to utter a kind of obscenity.

I dutifully sign petitions, call
"elected representatives", send
paltry checks to charities I admire,

as fatalism hovers at my mind's edge,
along with guilt at my uselessness.
I ask myself for the hundredth time:

Is poetry a trivial pursuit?
A mere self-centered exercise?
A vocation become irrelevant

when society stuffs its maw
with scandal, porn and violence?
Yet even as I ask my eye is drawn

to branches bowing low in the breeze –
the big black oak behind my house,
older than any human still alive.

Layers of leaves like flirtatious ruffles
dancing in slanted sunlight. Dark rutted trunk.
Roots grown deeper than graves.

Why should it be this that makes me cry?
   And should I
      write about it?

Arithmetic

What does it all add up to?
To Adam add Eve,
plus two more, Cain and Abel.
Add one murder,
subtract Abel.
Add to the remaining three, mother, father, son,
generations generated how, where, by whom unclear,
who multiply multiple times

to become the quantity subtracted
by the flood – Noah and his brood
the remainder,
who add to themselves for centuries,
becoming masses from which
to subtract *en masse,*
as at Auschwitz, Treblinka, Bergen-Belsen,
plus the *et ceteras* from which to subtract.

Calculate the subtractions
at Hiroshima and Nagasaki.
Add minuses at London and Dresden,
plus subtractions from unnumbered wars –
Korea, Viet Nam, Serbia, Rwanda,
Iraq, Syria, Lebanon, plus
all the *et ceteras* around the globe
from which to subtract,

as this day's carnage is added
to that of countless yesterdays:
Gallipoli, Verdun, the Somme.
Wounded Knee and similar
seldom-recalled *et ceteras.*

Back to Antietum. To Wars of the Roses.
Back to Alexander. To Sumer and Elam.
Beyond the reach of recorded history.
Millenia of slaughter, all the way back

to when weapons, primitive but effective,
were sticks and stones
for breaking arms and legs, crushing skulls.
Long before we learned how to count
our wars; before we learned how to write
about wars, or taught ourselves to forget
their horrors after a while
so we could start them all over again.

No mortal can calculate all the subtractions –
each a human being – since it all began.
So I ask the god in whom I would like to believe
to do the math and tell us please:

    What does it all add up to?

Out of the Night

After fitful sleep she wakes before dawn,
looks out the window of her dark room,
waits for the dream still clinging to her skin
to lose its grip. It is slipping from her memory
but has a hold on her body.
Death was a theme, she remembers that.
Someone in danger, a matter of life and death.
Why couldn't she help?   Or
was she the one in danger with no one to help?
Her heart batters her rib cage.
Inhale, exhale.   Enough.

She looks to the east, where a slice of light,
orange as the centers of California poppies,
rims the tops of taupe-shadowed hills.
Soon the town in the dusky valley below
will rouse itself from sea-green slumbers
and punctuate leftover night with lighted windows.
Already she sees that this is a morning set
to blossom like a rose in a time-lapse film.
Looking like half-notes in this light,
juncos in the oaks begin their chatter.
They're birds, they're alive, and this is a new day.

She will write today but will not draw
on loss, loneliness or disasters,
natural or un – *un* as in carnage
wrought by humans to destroy
other humans. Especially not that.
She forbids death of any kind
to leak from the tip of her pen.

14th Autumn

—to Edna St. Vincent Millay for writing God's World

Certain that she, like marvelous Edna,
will one day burn her candle at both ends,
she unties her neat pony tail, wishes winds
might play in her long blond hair forever.

She sits and hugs her knees up on the hill
behind the junior high because from there
she can see below the entire town – small,
tidy, sweet. Trees waving colors of fire;

the bay's choppy waters by turns blue and gray.
O world, she begins, then starts to cry.
She recites God's World through tears, for she's undone
by glorious October and her hormones.

In May After Rain

You open your door, step into air
rinsed to a shimmer, scented green.
A subtle blend – weeds grass leaves,
new again all of it
one more time,
how many times again
an open question.
You step into post-rain stillness,
gentle beauty.

Grief, wholly unexpected,
squeezes your heart in its fist;
overcomes the Now, sends you back
to an almost-not-quite mem'ry
from your earliest years:
the once-upon in your life
before you came to know
that everyone who loved you
would not be with you always.

Rerun

—for my mother

The TV blinked erratic ice-blue flickers
at your unblinking eyes.
Sitcoms, newscasts, weather reports
(rain, it was April)
came and went for hours. Clamorous commercials
wheedled, coaxed, insisted
in demanding decibels, but failed to reach
your unhearing ears.

You slipped off the couch and out of your life while watching TV.

So ends your story, but of course its end
is hardly its *ending*.
If, as some say, it's all fiction
once it is written down,
I would not write your ending if I could –
not for a cheap sense of closure,
the cold comfort of a declarative.
I'd rather the unease,

the sad insufficiency of the interrogative:

Did you doze into death unaware?
Did your long-gone mother come and beckon you?
Were you in pain and afraid?
Did you grieve, in a last lucid moment,
at being all alone?

When Last I Held Your Hand

—for my father

Prodigious, your every ragged breath those final hours.
Each one heaved, hauled up
from some incalculable depth.
Your labor astonishing, its arduousness.
We your daughters, eldest and youngest,
marking at the last the seconds between –
forty-four   fifty   sixty-three –
scarcely breathing ourselves
in those liminal moments, needing,
as we believed for your sake,
to recognize exactly when.

A Coming To Mind

—for my mother

How we got there I don't know.
That's how it is with such things.
You, three weeks gone,
wore a dress I'd never seen,
and there we were in Venice.
No sun-washed piazza,
no haggling gondoliers.
Nowhere near the Bridge of Sighs.

Urgency was all over you
but you didn't speak a word.
You hurried me down an alley –
shadowy, snaking, too narrow I thought
for a good deep breath.
I wondered how you knew your way.
You never had been to that city.
We veered to an abrupt dead end.

There, at the nowhere-else-to-go,
a statue. A pale marble Jesus,
arms open as if to say,
Come unto Me. Or maybe,
What do you want this time? His face
suffused with compassion, or maybe
disappointment.
You wept.

For grief or joy, impossible to tell.
Or were they after all not tears
but seeping embalmer's brew. Your hair
was brown and full, as in your youth. I woke,
then instantly forgot the color of your dress.

That was decades ago. The dream does not haunt me,
but stays with me still. And still,
when it happens to come to mind,

I look for it to mean something.

Observance

—for Beatrice Abbott Duggan

Outside the sanctuary, like a constant
exhalation through clenched teeth, a high wind
humbles the trees. Shhhh. Admonishing.

Inside, we gather into small black flocks,
fluttering softly, feeling the tremors
of air charged white with loss and restraint.

She was the heart and soul of that family,
her old friend sighs. *We thought he'd be the first
to go.* Our eyes turn furtive, seeking him.

                         Gaunt, bent
by illness, age and grief – oh he is
breathtaking. Luminous. Bones like carved

ivory beneath his thin, pearl flesh.
How he gleams in his obsidian suit;
gleams in his silent, perfect sorrow.

Seen silhouetted black before a pale
chancel window, he is shaped and spare
as a mystic glyph signifying *Bereft*.

Sculpted to an elegance, this man
was finished the instant the heart of the heart
and soul fell still. Long a work in progress,

he is a masterpiece now.

Heartsong

—for Lauri and Stephen

When you were yet a sea thing
and I the sea, I rocked you
here beneath my heart.

  pum-pum, pum-pum

Those were the days of your turning
into. Your undulant gyrings,
your slow wheelings 'round.

A gentle time of waves,
when you rode upon the tides
of my night sighs and stirrings;

of my daily to's and fro's
in a world I prayed,
with each beat of my heart,

  would be kind

to the dear beached creature
you soon would be,
when nine full moons had drawn you

to the ineluctable shore.

Bounty

—for Stephen and Yvette

After your apple-picking at Averill Farms,
my most capacious bowl, painted on the outside
with sunflowers, apples and pears, became
a small mountain of tumbled globes.
Autumn's colors resting cheek to cheek
on the kitchen table. Gold burnished with rose;
deep garnet; pink with sage-green striations;
lipstick red; and a perfect May-like green.
Each one blessing our October.

We ate them cut into wedges, different
varieties at once, to share and compare
their separate kinds of savoriness.
Like a wine tasting without formality
or pretension. Paired with cheddar
and good bread, or with nothing at all,
they were used up in our enjoyment
until one apple remained, the one we
seemed silently to agree to keep

for last; the one with a spray of leaves
still attached to make us remember
root and trunk, limb and branch, frilly blossoms
giving way to small hard knots that grow until
they fill a human hand; fill our ready mouths
with their thin leather skins, crunchy flesh,
juices tart or sugary. One last apple
to remind us, before we consume it,
of ordinary miracles.

Jasper

He is a big determined cat.
He and I have grown old together.
Overweight, arthritic, he still can manage
a short leap onto the couch where I sit,
my back against an armrest, my legs
stretched out along its length,
reading Robert Hass's *Human Wishes*.

He settles his bulk on my thighs –
my thighs and down to my shins;
he is long as well as wide –
and presses his face to the book.
When nose nudging gets him nowhere
he butts the book with his head.
This has become our ritual.

I set the book aside, kiss him on the head,
wipe the corners of his eyes,
and get on with the "heavy petting",
an expression that meant something else
when I was young. His purr so fills my ears
it might be an organ. I am aware
this touching feeds a hunger in us both.

I think of the fates of babies
in orphanages a century ago.
Never rocked or cuddled in anyone's arms,
touched only for a feeding or a diaper change,
most of them died in their first year of life.
They were not malnourished they were starved –
we know it now – for the human touch.

The cat beneath my hand has gone to sleep.
At his age his skin hangs slack,
but unlike some old cats and unlike me,
he has sprouted no white hairs. Instead,
his tabby markings, striking once,
are steadily darkening, like day
moving inexorably toward night.

Bestowals

Suppose there were a kiss with wings.
Suppose the kiss were at liberty,
independent of any claimant, free
to fly itself far or near, free
to bestow itself on whomever it pleased

whenever it pleased.
Suppose the kiss to be tender,
with a sense of humor, too.
It might light with equal affection
on the cheek of a child in a backyard swing

and the chin of a circus man
who shoots himself from a cannon;
might touch the fluff of a week-old chick
then land on the snout of an aardvark.
Probably this kiss

would pucker up for goldfish
and blowfish (assume the kiss could swim).
This kiss, it surely would tickle the ear
of anyone dancing for joy.
Certainly this kiss

would brush the brows of the dying;
graze the temples of those who moan
in the ravaged places of the earth;
the ravaged places of the heart.
This kiss

never would be caught in the act,
but now and then would leave,
on the souls of the perceptive
and those in greatest need,
a small but indelible mark.

Light

The soul says,
I am too much in the dark. I long
to glimpse my origins.
The eyes gaze
on a sunlit field of snow.
Near the fence a boulder lies
sheathed in ice.
Like Michelangelo's finger of God
pointing through light years,
sun rays touch
the humble chunk of granite.
Candescence blinds by its suddenness!
Mere seconds,
but fierce for the human eye,
as though light had exploded out of the heart
of the rock.
But the unblinking soul stirs,
fixes the instant in the mind's eye,
says, *I see.*

November 19th, 1:35 p.m.

In this moment I give thanks

for the sleek gray cat passing through the room
with his silence, his chartreuse eyes, his silken fur;

for a ray of sun on the philodendron, turning it splendid;
for philodendrons, which flourish with or without love;

for the cheery look of five bananas
on the counter in a chipped blue bowl;

for my broom and my dishcloth, humble items
which reveal results for my labors

when my pen and paper do not –
but also for pen and paper;

for the last rusty leaves dropping from the oaks
behind the house, and the squirrels playing in the oaks

(their acorn harvest done, fattened for winter,
they are less frenetic this month than last);

for the industrious roar of a blower down the block
as a neighbor rids his yard of leaves he welcomed in May;

for the old clock ticking off the days of my life,
steady through my sorrows and my joys.

In this moment I give thanks for these dear random things,
and for another day in this terrible beautiful world.

Take My Love

—for all whom I hold dear

It may be love will be my sole bequest.
My years accumulate, my fortunes fade.
But take my love and hold it to your breast.

When doubts beset you and you feel hard-pressed
to find a friend, and life seems but charade,
embrace my love if it's my sole bequest.

When all turns bright, when wishes manifest,
when fortune pours out wealth and accolade,
still take my love and hold it to your breast.

My dear ones watch, lest you become obsessed
with all that's fleeting, all that's bound to fade,
and know that love is still my soul's bequest.

Like me, you are but temporary guests
upon this earth, so sing your serenade!
Then take my love and hold it to your breast.

With gifts of joy and pain my life was blest.
I'll leave it as I entered, unafraid.
When I take leave I'll have but one request:
Embrace my love and hold it to your breast.

About the Author

Gae Alexander was born in her paternal grandparents' home outside Roosevelt, Utah and grew up in Shelton, Washington. She studied at Brigham Young University and Kirkland College, then sister school to Hamilton College, graduating with a B.A. in literature and theatre. She is also a graduate of the American Academy of Dramatic Arts in New York City. On joining Actors' Equity Association, she learned her name was too similar to that of another actor to be practical. She borrowed names from two ancestors and became Rebecca Dobson for professional purposes. In addition to acting she co-founded and served as Producing Artistic Director of American Kaleidoscope Theatre. She has taught both privately and at the Connecticut Conservatory of the Performing Arts. Although her career was theatre-based she has always had a passion for poetry and started writing it in earnest in the 1990's. She reads her work in venues in Connecticut and New York City. She is a member of the Connecticut Poetry Society and is active in the Danbury, CT Chapter. *My Side of The River* is her first book.